While My Guitar Gently Weeps

arranged for lever or pedal harp by Sylvia Woods

words and music by George Harr

T0087398

This sheet music includes three solo harp arrangements.

Page 1 - for lever harps tuned to the key of C or 1 flat

Page 3 - for lever harps tuned to 2 or 3 flats

Page 5 - for pedal harp

1

While My Guitar Gently Weeps
for lever harps tuned to the key of C or 1 flat

Words and music by GEORGE HARRISON
Arranged for harp by SYLVIA WOODS

Set your sharping levers for the key signature, and then set the levers shown above.

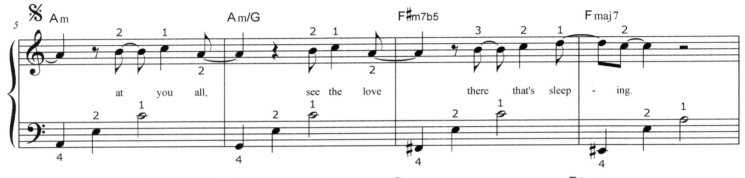

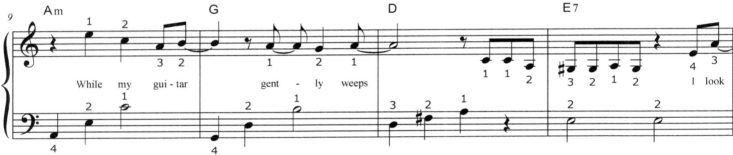

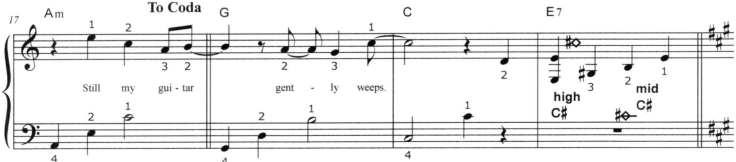

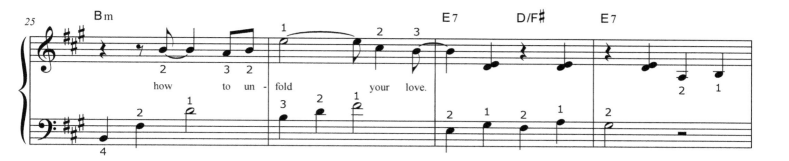

3

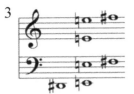

While My Guitar Gently Weeps

for lever harps tuned to 2 or 3 flats

Words and music by GEORGE HARRISON
Arranged for harp by SYLVIA WOODS

Set your sharping levers for the key signature, and then set the levers shown above.

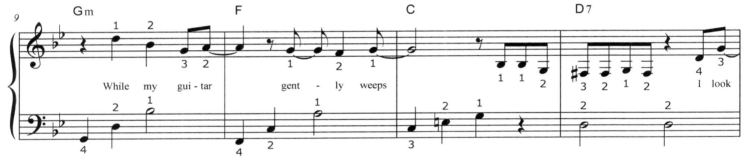

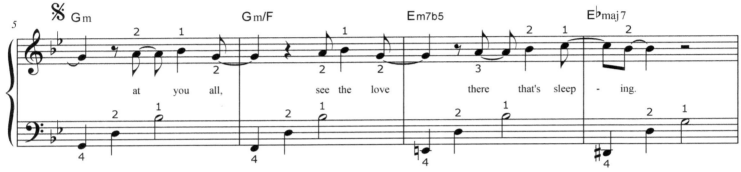

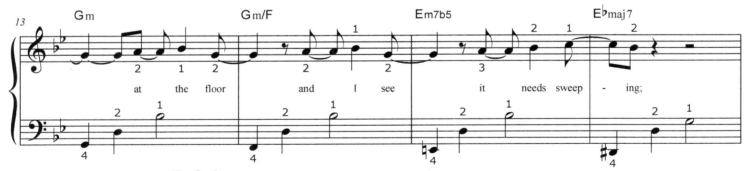

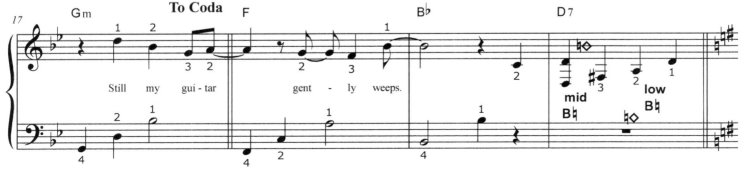

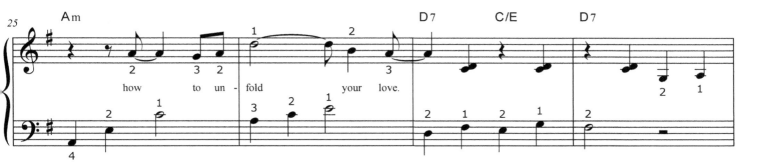

D.S. al Coda

While My Guitar Gently Weeps

for pedal harp

Words and music by GEORGE HARRISON
Arranged for harp by SYLVIA WOODS

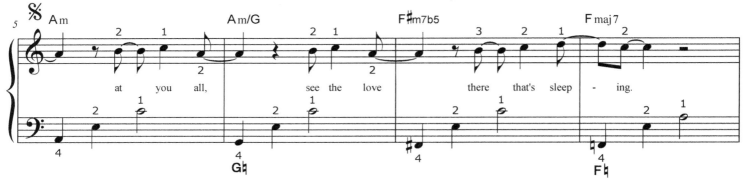

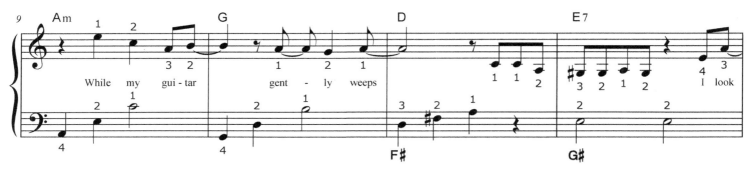

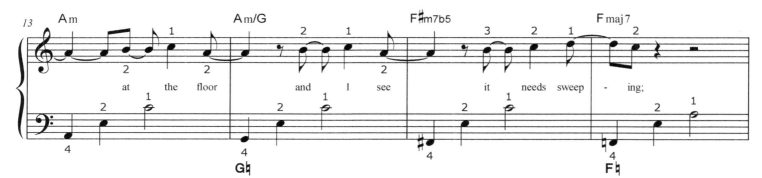

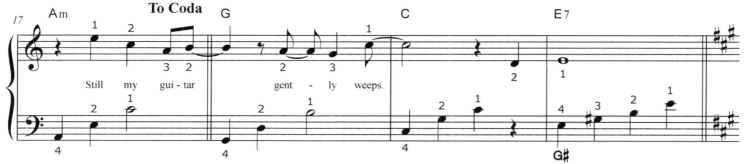

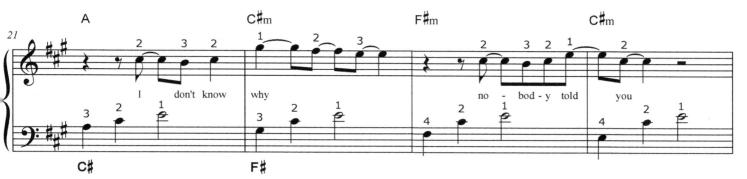

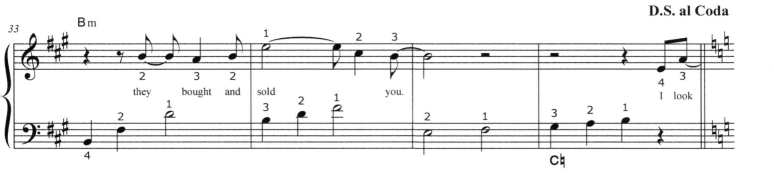

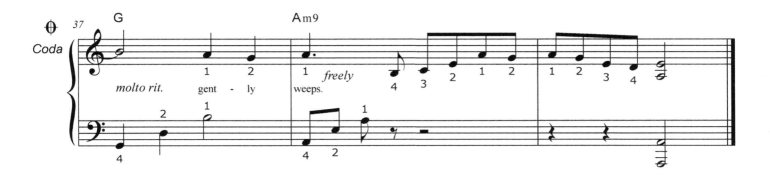

More harp arrangements by Sylvia Woods

Here Comes the Sun
by George Harrison

George Harrison's "Here Comes the Sun" was first released on the Beatles' 1969 "Abbey Road" album. Sylvia Woods has created three 4-page intermediate solo harp arrangements of this song, all included in one piece of sheet music. The arrangements are for lever harps tuned to the key of C, for lever harps tuned to flats, and for pedal harps. Lyrics, fingerings, and chord symbols are included. 12 pages of music.

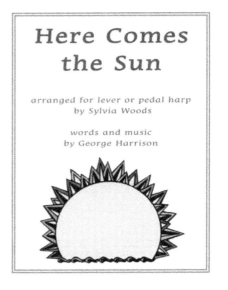

LENNON and McCARTNEY for the harp

46 of the most popular songs by John Lennon and Paul McCartney have been arranged for the harp by Sylvia Woods. The songs can be played on lever or pedal harp. For intermediate to advanced harp players.

Some of the pieces are quite easy, and others have extensive sharping lever or pedal changes. Lyrics, fingerings, and chord symbols are included. 144 pages.

Across The Universe	I've Just Seen A Face
All My Loving	Let It Be
All Together Now	Little Child
And I Love Her	The Long And Winding Road
Because	Michelle
Can't Buy Me Love	Mother Nature's Son
Eight Days A Week	Norwegian Wood
Eleanor Rigby	Not A Second Time
The Fool On The Hill	Nowhere Man
For No One	Ob-La-Di, Ob-La-Da
Get Back	Paperback Writer
Girl	Penny Lane
Golden Slumbers	Rain
Good Night	She's Leaving Home
Here, There And Everywhere	Thank You Girl
Hey Jude	This Boy
I Should Have Known Better	We Can Work It Out
I Will	With A Little Help From My Friends
If I Fell	Yellow Submarine
I'll Follow The Sun	Yes It Is
I'm Happy Just To Dance With You	Yesterday
I'm Looking Through You	You Won't See Me
In My Life	You've Got To Hide Your Love Away